WEST MIDLANDS RAILWAYS

from STEAM *to* MODERN TRACTION

PETER TUFFREY

GREAT NORTHERN

ACKNOWLEDGEMENTS

I am grateful for the help received from the following people: Roger Arnold, David Burrill, Paul Chancellor, John Chalcraft, David Christie, Michael Mercer, Hugh Parkin, Richard Postill, Bill Reed, Andrew, Rachel and Sue Warnes.

Gratitude should also be expressed to my son Tristram for his general help and encouragement throughout the course of the project.

Front Cover: Ivatt Class 2MT no. 41209 is pictured alongside a Class 120 DMU at Shrewsbury station during 1962. Photograph courtesy Colour-Rail.

Great Northern Books
PO Box 1380, Bradford, BD5 5FB
www.greatnorthernbooks.co.uk

ISBN: 978-1-914227-87-5

Design and layout: David Burrill

CIP Data
A catalogue for this book is available from the British Library

INTRODUCTION

The West Midlands was well-served by railways crossing the 5,000 square miles of territory. These included main lines, branches, connecting routes and industrial railways. In the wake of the 'Modernisation & Re-Equipment of British Railways' report of 1955 the area saw many changes which altered the rail system completely. Steam locomotives were quickly replaced with diesels and electrics, whilst lines and stations closed, others rebuilt and electrification schemes carried out. The period also coincided with the increased use of cameras which allowed enthusiasts to record their local scenes or visit from further afield. As a result, an important time in British transport history has been captured.

Several areas form the West Midlands Region: Herefordshire; Shropshire; Staffordshire; Warwickshire; Worcestershire; West Midlands County (created as part of the Local Government Act 1972). Cities include: Birmingham; Coventry; Hereford; Lichfield; Stoke-on-Trent; Wolverhampton; Worcester. Some of the towns are: Burton-on-Trent; Dudley; Kidderminster; Leamington Spa; Nuneaton; Rugby; Shrewsbury; Stafford; Stourbridge; Tamworth; Uttoxeter; etc.

Railway developments in the West Midlands were spurred by the Industrial Revolution and the Stockton & Darlington and Liverpool & Manchester Railways. The Grand Junction Railway was promoted in the early 1830s and able to connect with the latter when opened in 1837 using the Warrington & Newton Railway, which had been active from 1831. The final section which completed this early major inter-city network was the London & Birmingham Railway. Though the idea for the route was developed in the 1820s, support was not gained until the 1830s and construction took around five years. The official opening occurred on 17th September 1838.

With this important network in place, smaller schemes began to join the route for local and national traffic. In the face of competition from the Great Western Railway, the original companies that formed part of the West Coast Main Line decided to create the London & North Western Railway. Despite becoming one of the most powerful companies in the country at the time, this was not enough to stop the GWR's expansion. The company was able to take over a number of schemes that led northwards through Birmingham and Wolverhampton to reach Birkenhead. Though the GWR had a dominant position for traffic westwards to Worcester, Kidderminster and Shrewsbury, there was some competition to the company from the Midland Railway which was able to make Gloucester and Bristol thanks to acquisitions during the 1840s.

The North Staffordshire Railway was a smaller company able to establish a network around Stoke-on-Trent. Unbelievably, a rail connection to this centre for pottery production was absent, leading to the NSR's formation in the mid-1840s. A route was authorised to run from Congleton to Stoke-on-Trent and Colwich, meeting the Trent Valley Railway. A second scheme saw a line laid from North Rode (near Macclesfield) to Burton-on-Trent via Uttoxeter. There were also branches to Crewe and Sandbach. When fully operational, the NSR had 216 route miles and managed to remain independent until the Grouping of 1923 when amalgamated with the LNWR and MR to form the London Midland & Scottish Railway.

In the 1920s and 1930s, the LMSR maintained the company's strong position around the West Midlands. This was despite a relative weakness in the locomotive stock. Before Grouping, the LNWR and MR had struggled to introduce successful passenger locomotives and the production of a new design was important by the mid-1920s. Despite being rivals, the GWR allowed the LMSR access to the new 'Castle' Class 4-6-0 and this resulted in Fowler creating the 'Royal Scot' Class which handled many passenger services running in the West Midlands to British Railways' days. A revolution in LMSR locomotive design occurred when W.A. Stanier (later Sir) was appointed Chief Mechanical Engineer of the LMSR in the early 1930s and over the next decade or so many of the familiar classes working around the area were created. These included: Class 5 4-6-0; 'Jubilee' 4-6-0; 8F Class 2-8-0; 'Princess Royal' and 'Coronation' Class Pacifics.

The GWR had been well-served by G.J. Churchward in the early 20th century and his successor Charles Collett followed this example. As mentioned, one of his first designs was the 'Castle' 4-6-0 and production continued steadily to create 155 examples, with a small number of rebuilds augmenting the fleet. Also built during the 1920s and 1930s were: 'Hall' Class 4-6-0s; 'King' Class 4-6-0s; 'Grange' Class 4-6-0s; 'Manor' Class 4-6-0s; 2884 Class 2-8-0s; 2251 Class 0-6-0s; 5101 Class 2-6-2Ts; 5700 and 8750 Class 0-6-0PTs; 1400 Class 0-4-2Ts. Latterly, Hawksworth's 'Modified Hall' Class 4-6-0s, 'County' Class 4-6-0s and 9400 Class 0-6-0PTs could be found on GWR lines.

As had been the case for the First World War, the Government took control of the railways in Britain when war was declared in 1939. The conflict placed a great strain on the rolling stock and infrastructure leaving the 'Big Four' likely unable to meet the arrears of repairs and maintenance when the war ended. Whereas Nationalisation was dismissed in favour of the Grouping, the position of the railways and political climate of the country in 1945 saw the idea of state control of the system possible. The Labour Party swept to power on such an agenda, starting with coal and electricity from 1947, followed by the railways in 1948 and steel in 1949.

The Transport Act 1947 created the British Transport Commission to oversee all forms of transport in Britain and Northern Ireland, including road haulage, bus companies, shipping firms, ports and the railways. From 1st January 1948, British Railways was responsible for the 'Big Four' companies which were split into regions. The West Midlands saw the lines divided between the London Midland Region and Western Region which were successors to the LMSR and GWR respectively.

At the time of BR's formation, there was little practical experience of diesel traction in Britain. The 'Big Four' had all experimented with shunters and some main line locomotives were completed at Nationalisation but were still under evaluation. The GWR introduced a fleet of diesel railcars from the early 1930s to early 1940s, whilst the LMSR ordered a number of diesel shunters from the trade over the same period. Before Nationalisation, the LMSR built two prototype main line diesel locomotives, nos 10000 and 10001, using English Electric components and these were being tested when locomotive policy was being developed post-1948.

In 1948, there were just over 20,000 locomotives constructed to nearly 450 different designs running in Britain. Though diesel and electric traction offered many benefits over steam, the decision was made to continue with steam and introduce several standardised classes to modernise the fleet, improve efficiency and simplify maintenance practices. Nearly 1,500 steam locomotives were built in the 1950s to work across the national network and reduce these numbers. Several types were introduced to the West Midlands, including the Standard Class 5 4-6-0, 9F 2-10-0, etc.

During the early 1950s, passenger numbers were relatively steady and freight traffic was only slightly declining. Yet, expenditure on infrastructure, rolling stock maintenance and replacement was heavy. The business lost money and caused concern, especially to the politicians overseeing BR. The railways had to compete for Treasury Funds with other areas and hope that national fortunes were such to allow spending to be authorised. Furthermore, the Labour Government fell to the Conservatives in the early 1950s and a fresh scrutiny was placed on the endeavour. A damaging feature of the Government's 1953 Transport Act was the divestment of all road haulage businesses and restrictions which contributed to the terminal decline of small-load freight traffic from the mid-1950s.

As a result, a committee was formed to examine the motive power options for BR and reported that dieselisation was favourable to shunting duties and local line services in the form of railcars, whilst a main line electrification scheme was desirable. With this information, a comprehensive report was assembled in 1954 to set out a long-term strategy. 'The Modernisation and Re-Equipment of British Railways' was published during January 1955 and called for £1.2 billion to be loaned by the Government. This was for the replacement of the steam fleet with new diesel locomotives, electrification of part of the West Coast Main Line, improved carriages and wagons, complete reorganisation of freight yards, resignalling and track improvements, and reconstruction of some stations.

In May 1955, BR began the Pilot Scheme for diesel locomotives, ordering Types according to power classifications. Also, several classes of Diesel Multiple Units were authorised for construction, with some tailored for specific areas. During 1957, the first Pilot Scheme orders started to be fulfilled and BR continued to receive the stock up to the end of the 1950s.

The West Midlands was a particularly interesting area at this time as many of these new types could be seen in the area. The striking English Electric Type 5 no. DP1 *Deltic* was trialled initially on the West Coast Main Line, as was the Associated Electrical Industries Type 4 no. D0260 *Lion*. More common varieties were the Sulzer Type 2s (Class 24 and 25), Brush Type 2 (Class 30, later 31), English Electric Type 4 (Class 40), Derby Type 4 (Classes 44, 45 and 46), and Brush Type 4 (Class 47), etc. The Western Region broke from the others by favouring diesel-hydraulic transmission instead of diesel electric. This resulted in a group of locomotives different from what was standard and these later became early casualties of an attempt to rationalise BR's locomotive fleet in the 1970s. With the electrification being carried out, the AL electric classes began working through the region and several stations were rebuilt to accommodate the new infrastructure.

In the early 1960s, Dr Richard Beeching was appointed to British Railways in order to improve fortunes. He felt that a good deal of the losses was the result of unprofitable lines leftover from the development of the railways. His report, 'The Reshaping of British Railways', appeared in March 1963 and called for 6,000 miles of lines with over 2,000 stations to close. The West Midlands was affected in many ways, with one of the major lines to be cut being the GWR route through the area to Birkenhead. This proved shortsighted as some of the trackbed has been resurrected as the West Midlands Metro.

Nearly 60 years from the end of steam in Britain and the transition to modern traction, the period is very interesting to look back on. Thankfully, many people were attentive enough at the time to capture the excellent photographs featured in this collection. Just as steam locomotives were saved at the time, many of the early diesels, DMUs, etc, also have been stopped from entering the scrapyard. Working side by side again at preservation sites around the country, they serve as a reminder of an important time in British history.

Peter Tuffrey

Doncaster, June 2025

Above ALVELEY COLLIERY – NO. 1420

The first locomotive to be preserved was *Locomotion No. 1* which hauled the first passenger train on the Stockton & Darlington Railway. Saved in the mid-1850s, just over a century later more were being diverted away from the scrapyard. Three of these locomotives were brought together to work the 'Restored Engines Tour' on 19th September 1965. The Midland branch of the Stephenson Locomotive Society obtained the services of Gresley K4 Class 2-6-0 no. 3442 *The Great Marquess*, Collett 1400 Class 0-4-2T no. 1420 and Churchward 4500 Class 2-6-2T no. 4555. No. 3442 started the day at Birmingham Snow Hill station and travelled to Worcester where the train was handed over to no. 1420 and no. 4555. The two engines took the party to Alveley Colliery sidings before returning southwards to Kidderminster. From there, the train went to Wolverhampton before following the same route back Birmingham Snow Hill, though without the colliery detour. No. 1420 is pictured at the latter and had been withdrawn nearly a year earlier. Presently, the locomotive is out of service for an overhaul at the South Devon Railway. Photograph by Richard Postill.

Above ASHFORD BOWDLER – NO. 7034
Charles Collett's 'Castle' Class 4-6-0 design was built over 27 years. The final ten engines were delivered from Swindon between May and August 1950, with no. 7034 *Ince Castle* amongst the number when completed. New to Bristol Bath Road shed, the locomotive was a year old when captured passing Ashford Bowdler with the 16.30 Bristol to Manchester express. No. 7034 was in traffic for 15 years. Photograph by C.R.L. Coles from Rail Archive Stephenson courtesy Rail-Online.

Opposite ASHFORD BOWDLER CROSSING
Two connecting railway schemes received authorisation in 1846. These were the Hereford & Shrewsbury Railway and Newport, Abergavenny & Hereford Railway. Both took seven years to complete and the first mentioned passed through the small village of Ashford Bowdler, south of Ludlow. A station was provided in 1854 but this lasted only a year. The railway cut over the road through the village to St Andrew's Church and a level crossing was installed. The keeper has been pictured at work during 1951. In the last decade, there was a plan to close the crossing but this was dismissed and safety improvements carried out instead. Photograph by C.R.L. Coles from Rail Archive Stephenson courtesy Rail-Online.

Above ASTON STATION – NO. D5082
An express freight travelling northwards approaches Aston station during May 1962. Brush Type 2 (Class 24) no. D5082 is at the head of the train. New to the Eastern Region, the locomotive soon transferred to the London Midland Region. In May 1962, no. D5082 was at Willesden for the first half of the month, though moved on to Watford for the second part and served there for over six months. Photograph courtesy Rail-Online.

Opposite above ASTON SHED – NO. 5733
Stanier 'Jubilee' Class 4-6-0 no. 5733 *Novelty* is at Aston shed for servicing on 30th March 1946. Ten years old at the time, the locomotive was in traffic nearly 28 years. Photograph by B.W.L. Brooksbank.

Opposite below ASTON SHED – NO. 2616
Outside Aston shed on 30th March 1946 is Stanier 4P Class 2-6-4T no. 2616. The engine had a long-term allocation to the depot. Photograph by B.W.L. Brooksbank.

6733

2616
L M S

7K28

Above ATHERSTONE – NO. 45555

An independent company decided to bypass Birmingham and reduce the distance for direct northbound trains. The Trent Valley Railway was authorised in 1845 and started work by the end of the year. During 1846, the TVR was taken over by the London & Birmingham Railway and just two months later, the LNWR was formed. The company continued the project which was completed fully in late 1847. As part of the West Coast Main Line electrification, the Trent Valley Line was also dealt with and the gantries are present here on 21st July 1962. Stanier 'Jubilee' Class 4-6-0 no. 45555 *Quebec* is seen passing Atherstone with the 12.20 Llandudno to Euston service. Photograph by Tony Cooke courtesy Colour-Rail.

Opposite ATHERSTONE – NO. E3129

After the announcement of the electrification scheme for the West Coast Main Line, BR placed orders for electric locomotives at several manufacturers to evaluate designs suitable for production. From this information, the AL6 (Class 86) was produced, numbering 100 examples. Amongst the group was no. E3129 which has a northbound freight to Stoke-on-Trent at Atherstone (south east of Tamworth) on 17th July 1968. In the early 2010s a Bulgarian rail operator bought surplus Class 87s, then later took six Class 86s, and this included no. E3129, then known as no. 86701. Photograph courtesy Rail-Online.

BARNT GREEN
B5
5

Above BARNT GREEN STATION – NO. 42764

When the Birmingham & Gloucester Railway passed through Barnt Green, north of Bromsgrove, in 1841 the company omitted to provide a station. By the middle of the decade, a facility was in place and later became the departure point for the branch to Redditch. Subsequently, this line was extended to Evesham and rejoined the Gloucester line at Ashchurch. Hughes 'Crab' Class 2-6-0 no. 42764 has a local train at Barnt Green station in April 1960. Based at Saltley shed, the locomotive was in service there until condemned during January 1962. Photograph courtesy Rail-Online.

Opposite BARNT GREEN STATION

In the early 1950s, a report produced for BR recommended replacing push-and-pull services on local lines with Diesel Multiple Units. Following early prototypes, BR ordered a number from the trade, especially following the 'Modernisation Plan'. Park Royal Vehicles, an established coachbuilder, supplied 20 two-car sets (Class 103) from November 1957 to October 1958. The units consisted of a Driving Motor Brake Second and Driving Trailer Composite Lavatory. All were delivered to the London Midland Region and seven had initial allocations to Walsall. One of the depot's units is seen at Barnt Green station during 1960. Photograph courtesy Colour-Rail.

49045

Above BESCOT – NO. D291
Travelling away from Bescot station (visible in the background) is English Electric Type 4 (Class 40) no. D291. The Grand Junction Railway opened a station nearby in 1837, though the LNWR built on the present site 13 years later. Since 1990, the facility has been known as Bescot Stadium to serve the home of Walsall Football Club. No. D291 was erected at Vulcan Foundry in August 1960 and had a career lasting 24 years. Photograph courtesy Colour-Rail.

Opposite above BESCOT – NO. 9171
The LNWR developed freight locomotives with an eight-coupled wheel arrangement over a number of years. The G1 Class of the early 20th century was a progression of the G Class and had a superheater, whilst also using piston valves. Numbering 171 new locomotives, the G1 Class also had older designs rebuilt to the specifications. No. 9171 was amongst the original class members and Crewe erected the engine in May 1912. At Bescot on 24th March 1951, no. 9171 has a Walsall to Wednesbury freight train. The locomotive had just a year left in service and the BR number was not applied before withdrawal. Photograph by B.W.L. Brooksbank.

Opposite below BESCOT – NO. 49045
Francis Webb experimented with compound expansion during his tenure with the LNWR. At the end of the 19th century over 100 A Class 0-8-0 three-cylinder compounds appeared from Crewe Works. Unfortunately, these proved inferior to the standard expected and Webb's successor George Whale began a reconstruction programme. No. 49045 was built in November 1897, then became a D Class 0-8-0, with new boiler and two cylinders, during April 1908. Under the LMSR, many older 0-8-0s were rebuilt to G2 specifications, though formed the G2A Class. No. 49045 initially went to the G1 Class in 1930, but at the end of the decade was placed in G2A. The locomotive is at Bescot on 24th March 1951. Photograph by B.W.L. Brooksbank.

BEWDLEY
2
3

Above BEWDLEY STATION – NO. 41240

After the Second World War, H.G. Ivatt produced the Class 2MT 2-6-2T design to replace some of the older and run-down locomotives in the LMSR fleet. From 1946 to 1952, 130 engines were built, mostly at Crewe Works. Though intended for the LMSR's local duties, following Nationalisation a number went to the Southern Region and later worked on the Western Region. No. 41240 was in service from September 1949 to September 1963. The locomotive is at Bewdley station on 27th October 1962 and had recently transferred to Shrewsbury shed from Bristol. Photograph courtesy Colour-Rail.

Opposite BEWDLEY STATION

The Severn Valley Railway connected Hartlebury with Shrewsbury and opened during 1862. Bewdley station was built at the time and the line was run by the West Midlands Railway, though this lasted just over a year before absorbed by the Great Western Railway. In 1864, Bewdley was the point of connection for the Tenbury branch. This image was captured c. 1960 and has a GWR railcar present. Bewdley station survived to 1970 but later became part of the Severn Valley Railway heritage line. Photograph courtesy Colour-Rail.

Above BILSTON – NO. D1005
The Western Region of BR broke away from the other areas in ordering diesel-hydraulic locomotives rather than diesel-electric. In the Type 4 power category, 74 locomotives (TOPS Class 52) were built at Swindon and Crewe between 1961 and 1964. No. D1005 *Western Venturer* was amongst the group and completed in June 1962. Just three months after this date, no. D1005 has an express running through Bilston. Photograph by B.W.L. Brooksbank.

Opposite above BILSTON CENTRAL STATION
Two companies were promoted to connect Oxford and Wolverhampton in the mid-1840s. When authorised, the GWR was interested in taking over the project and this occurred during 1847. The southern section from Oxford to Birmingham was completed first, then the line to Wolverhampton was ready for traffic in 1854. Bilston Central station opened at this time and was in use to 1972. This view dates from 4th September 1962. Photograph by B.W.L. Brooksbank.

Opposite below BILSTON WEST STATION
Although a project was underway to join Oxford with Wolverhampton, another company, the Oxford, Worcester & Wolverhampton Railway, took a westerly route and reached completion in the early 1850s. Bilston West station opened during 1854 and closed a few months before pictured on 4th September 1962. Photograph by B.W.L. Brooksbank.

BILSTON CENTRAL STATION

BIRMINGHAM NEW STREET STATION
BR Class AM10 (TOPS Class 310) no. 310089 stands next to AL1 (Class 81) no. E3003 at Birmingham New Street during July 1967. Photograph by Richard Postill.

Above BIRMINGHAM NEW STREET STATION – NO. 61323
An uncommon visitor to Birmingham New Street station is Thompson B1 Class 4-6-0 no. 61323. The locomotive is making an empty stock movement after working the 13.42 train from Peterborough East via Rugby on 14th April 1960. Photograph by B.W.L. Brooksbank.

Below BIRMINGHAM NEW STREET STATION – NO. 44859
Stanier Class 5 no. 44859 has an eastbound train of empty stock leaving Birmingham New Street station on 7th August 1965. Photograph by B.W.L. Brooksbank.

8109

TAYLOR & CHALLEN LTD.
D1699
1V04

Above BIRMINGHAM SNOW HILL STATION – NO. D1072

In as-built condition at Birmingham Snow Hill station during late 1963 is Western Type 4 (Class 52) no. D1072 *Western Glory*. The locomotive had three years working from Old Oak Common before transferring into the West Country, first at Plymouth, then Bristol before returning to Plymouth. No. D1072 was condemned there during November 1976. Photograph by Richard Postill.

Opposite above BIRMINGHAM SNOW HILL STATION – NO. 8109

In the early 20th century, G.J. Churchward adopted the 2-6-2T wheel arrangement for a locomotive class to be used on suburban services. After experience with a prototype, 39 more engines were built at Swindon during 1905 and 1906. Forming the 3100 Class, no. 8109 was amongst the group when completed in February 1905 as no. 3115. From the late 1920s, the class saw modifications carried out and the locomotives were renumbered as a result becoming the 5100 Class. No. 3115 became no. 5115 in 1928, then just before the Second World War had this altered again to no. 8109. The change was due to ten class members being given smaller diameter wheels and higher boiler pressure for improved acceleration when working London suburban services. These 8100 Class engines did not prove much better than standard and were redistributed subsequently. No. 8109 was in the middle of an allocation to Tyseley when pictured at Birmingham Snow Hill station on 29th September 1962. The locomotive was in service to June 1965. Photograph by Richard Postill.

Opposite below BIRMINGHAM SNOW HILL STATION – NO. D1699

Brush Type 4 (Class 47) no. D1699 is at Birmingham Snow Hill station on 13th March 1964. The locomotive was new from Brush Traction in December 1963 and delivered to Old Oak Common shed. After 18 months there, no. D1699 moved on to Bristol. Photograph by Richard Postill.

Above BIRMINGHAM SNOW HILL STATION – NO. 5350
The 11.45 service from Swansea High Street to Birmingham Snow Hill arrives at the station behind Churchward 4300 Class 2-6-0 no. 5350 on 10th August 1957. The locomotive was amongst 65 class members modified to carry extra weight at the front end to stabilise the pony truck. This resulted in reclassification to the 8300 Class. Yet, wartime engine availability meant the weights had to be removed and the class reverted to 4300. No. 5350 was in traffic to December 1959. Photograph by B.W.L. Brooksbank.

Opposite above BIRMINGHAM SNOW HILL STATION
Serving the GWR's operations in Birmingham, Snow Hill station was open from 1852 to 1972 as the ex-LNWR lines were favoured. Yet, the facility was resurrected in 1987 and now also hosts the West Midlands Metro. This image shows the station in a run-down condition on 2nd March 1972. Photograph by Richard Postill.

Opposite below BIRMINGHAM SNOW HILL STATION
A Class 122 DMU is at Birmingham Snow Hill station with the service to Stourbridge Town on 2nd March 1972. From 1966 trains had been diverted to New Street and inter-city services ceased the following year. After closure in 1972, the station was used as a car park, then demolished. Photograph by Richard Postill.

TOWN
TV054
B2

1Z65
TRAIN
A
M9206
GREAT WESTERN

Above BIRMINGHAM SNOW HILL STATION – NO. W25W
In the mid-1930s, the GWR introduced a diesel railcar which led to a class of 38 vehicles. No. W25W was part of a group built at Swindon in the early 1940s. Whilst the early examples were designed to run singly, later railcars had the ability to connect with other carriages and wagons, whilst the last ones were joined together as an early form of DMU. At Birmingham Snow Hill station during March 1953, no. W25W has a service from Dudley which features a compartment brake carriage for extra capacity. Photograph courtesy Rail-Online.

Opposite above BIRMINGHAM – NO. 10000
Shortly after the Second World War ended, the LMSR decided to trial diesel traction on main line services. Under H.G. Ivatt, the company entered an agreement with English Electric to produce two 1,650 horsepower locomotives, with the LMSR to supply many components and EE the engine and traction motors, etc. No. 10000 was completed at the end of 1947 and no. 10001 appeared during the following year. Both worked apart and together to produce a number of impressive performances on both passenger and freight duties. The locomotives were in service for around 15 years before withdrawn and scrapped. In the 1950s, no. 10000 has been caught on the Birmingham Avoiding Line (between Aston and Stechford) with an express. Photograph courtesy Rail-Online.

Opposite below BIRMINGHAM SNOW HILL STATION – NO. 7029
In early March 1967, the GWR's route from Wolverhampton to Birkenhead was taken out of use. The Midland Branch of the Stephenson Locomotive Society commemorated this event with two special trains. One was led by recently preserved Collett 'Castle' Class 4-6-0 no. 7029 *Clun Castle*, whilst the other had Stanier Class 5 no. 44680 in charge. Two BR Standard Class 9F 2-10-0s also appeared on the trains, running between Chester and Birkenhead. For the return to Birmingham Snow Hill, the 4-6-0s switched the trains worked on the northbound journey. No. 7029 is seen before the departure from Snow Hill station. Photograph by Bill Wright courtesy Michael Mercer.

106
D6943

Above BLACKWELL – NO. 44569
Blackwell was at the summit of Lickey Incline and a station also stood there. There were sidings for assisting locomotives and freight trains had to pause for testing the brakes before descending for the prevention of runaways. Fowler 4F Class 0-6-0 no. 44569 has reached Blackwell with a freight service on 14th April 1949. Built at Crewe Works in August 1937, the BR number was applied from November 1948. The engine was a long-term servant at Bristol. Withdrawal occurred in July 1964. Photograph by B.W.L. Brooksbank.

Opposite BLACKWELL – NO. D6943 AND NO. D6833
BR needed a locomotive with a Type 3 (1,500 to 2,000 horsepower) rating and English Electric was able to supply a design (TOPS Class 37) based on locomotives the company had already built. This was accepted and BR placed an initial order for 42 in 1959. Further batches were built up to 1965 when 309 had entered traffic. No. D6943 was a late example and completed by Vulcan Foundry in September 1964. The locomotive is at Blackwell after completing the climb on the Lickey Incline with a freight train during 1965. Assisting is no. D6833, which had been constructed by English Electric in April 1963. Both were in service to the early 2000s. Photograph courtesy Colour-Rail.

80102

Above BRIDGNORTH STATION
By the late 1950s, the original GWR railcars were becoming life expired and BR introduced the Class 122 units to replace them on the WR local services. The Gloucester Railway Carriage & Wagon Co. supplied 20 motor vehicles as well as nine trailers during 1958. One of the Driving Motor Brake Seconds has made a stop at Bridgnorth station on 13th April 1963. Some Class 122 vehicles saw further use in Departmental Stock and eight driving units have been preserved. Photograph courtesy Colour-Rail.

Opposite BRIDGNORTH STATION – NO. 80102
The LMSR had a group of 2-6-4T locomotives that worked local and secondary passenger duties and BR decided to base the Standard Class 4MT on the latest Fairburn development. Between 1951 and 1956, 155 engines were produced, mainly at Brighton, though small batches appeared from Derby and Doncaster. No. 80102 was the product of Brighton in March 1955 and delivered to Plaistow. By the time of this image, 13th April 1963, the locomotive had relocated to Shrewsbury shed via a few other depots. No. 80102 has a local train at Bridgnorth station a few months before closure. The facility has been resurrected as part of the Severn Valley Railway. The locomotive moved on to the Southern Region in mid-1965 and had six months there before condemned for scrap. Photograph courtesy Colour-Rail.

BROMSGROVE STATION – NO. D35

Derby Type 4 (Class 45) no. D35 passes Bromsgrove station on 5th April 1964. Photograph by K.C.H. Fairey courtesy Colour-Rail.

Above BROMSGROVE STATION – NO. 5568
A Bradford to Paignton express has reached Bromsgrove with Stanier 'Jubilee' Class no. 5568 *Western Australia* on 24th July 1948. Photograph by B.W.L. Brooksbank.

Below BROMSGROVE STATION – NO. D7001
Beyer, Peacock & Co. Type 3 (Class 35) no. D7001 takes the through line at Bromsgrove station on 23rd September 1964. Photograph courtesy Colour-Rail.

42818

3/46
FRI SPL

Above BURTON-ON-TRENT – NO. 73130
Several attempts were made to harness the advantages of poppet valves. In the early 1950s, BR modified the Caprotti design and equipped two Stanier Class 5s, then following this up with a group of 30 BR Standard Class 5 4-6-0s. One of these engines, no. 73130, has a special service at Burton-on-Trent on 30th June 1962. The locomotive was first allocated to Shrewsbury in September 1956, but moved on to Patricroft two years later. Withdrawal from there occurred in January 1967. Photograph by John Briggs courtesy A1 Steam Trust.

Opposite above BURTON-ON-TRENT – NO. 42818
A small group of Hughes 'Crab' Class 2-6-0 locomotives were fitted with Lentz poppet valves and rotary cam valve gear in the early 1930s. The advantage of this was significantly reduced wear when compared to piston valves and improved valve events. No. 42818, which has a short freight at Burton-on-Trent on 18th June 1957, was a recipient, though in the early 1950s the type was changed to Reidinger. Photograph by B.W.L. Brooksbank.

Opposite below BURTON-ON-TRENT STATION – NO. 44235
Whilst the 'North Midlands Rail Tour' changed engines at Burton-on-Trent station on 11th May 1963, Fowler 4F Class 0-6-0 no. 44235 passes through the crowd with a coal train. Photograph by B.W.L. Brooksbank.

41328

Above BURTON-ON-TRENT – NO. D6603
English Electric Type 3 (Class 37) no. D6603 had been completed recently at Vulcan Foundry when pictured at Burton-on-Trent during late 1965. The locomotive was new to Landore, Swansea, and spent a number of years in South Wales. Withdrawal occurred during 1997. Photograph by Bill Wright courtesy Michael Mercer.

Opposite BURTON-ON-TRENT – NO. 41328
Ivatt Class 2MT 2-6-2T no. 41328 has the Tutbury push-and-pull at Burton-on-Trent station, c. 1960. Photograph by Bill Reed.

BURTON - ON
M985
A
S·L·S SPECIAL
BURTON-ON-TRENT

Above BURTON-ON-TRENT – NO. 48271

Light engine at Burton-on-Trent in the mid-1960s is Stanier 8F Class 2-8-0 no. 48271. Built by the North British Locomotive Company for the War Department in June 1942, the locomotive was purchased by the LMSR during the following year becoming no. 8271. Under BR, the engine worked in the Midlands at Toton for 11 years, then moving on to Burton-on-Trent. After three years, no. 48271 made a final transfer to Northwich and withdrawal occurred during August 1967. Photograph by Bill Wright courtesy Michael Mercer.

Opposite BURTON-ON-TRENT STATION

The 'North Staffordshire & Crompton & High Peak Rail Tour' was arranged by the Stephenson Locomotive Society's Midland Area branch to run on the 15th April 1961. The point of departure was Burton-on-Trent and a Class 105 DMU is ready to start the day there. Making their way to Parsley Hay, Riddles J94 Class 0-6-0ST no. 68013 was waiting for the party and took the train to Hopton Top. Class mate no. 68030 joined in on the ascent to Middleton Top. The excursion ended with a journey from Wirksworth to Derby. Photograph courtesy Colour-Rail.

44744

16

Above CASTLE BROMWICH STATION

The British Industries Fair was held from 1915 to 1957 and starting in 1920 Castle Bromwich was a venue for the event. The station there, which had opened in 1842, was close to the purpose-built exhibition centre and the point of departure for visitors, with a multi-lingual sign advertising the fact on the left. To highlight the capabilities of Metropolitan-Cammell, new Class 101 DMUs were in use for passengers. The vehicle is under the scrutiny of three gentlemen here during April 1956. When the fair ended, the exhibition hall was cleared and a housing estate built on the site. Castle Bromwich station closed in 1968, though plans are in place to establish a new facility. Photograph courtesy Rail-Online.

Opposite above CASTLE BROMWICH – NO. 44744

Before British Caprotti valve gear was fitted to the BR Standard Class 5s, 20 Stanier Class 5s were tested with the equipment. No. 44744 was part of the group and completed at Crewe Works in July 1948. The locomotives differed from later examples in having the drive for the poppet valves placed between the frames and operated by gearing connected to the leading coupled axle. No. 44744 has a northbound express at Castle Bromwich during July 1955 when based at Bristol Barrow Road shed. The engine was in service to November 1963. Photograph courtesy Rail-Online.

Opposite below CASTLE BROMWICH – NO. D51

From the LMSR main line diesel design, BR developed the Derby Type 4 (Classes 44, 45 and 46). A total of 192 locomotives were erected, though differences of engine and traction motor resulted in a segregation to three classes under TOPS. No. D51 was built at Crewe during June 1962 and had a 2,500 horsepower Sulzer 12LDA28B engine, which was intercooled. This latter placed the locomotive in Class 45 along with 127 others. No. D51 has a train at Castle Bromwich in the mid-1960s. Photograph courtesy Rail-Online.

Above CHATTERLEY – NO. 45297

Just north of Stoke-on-Trent, a station was built on the line to Macclesfield for the town of Tunstall in 1864. This was not well-sited for the settlement, so the North Staffordshire Railway opened a loop around a decade later. The original station was renamed Chatterley but then became unnecessary and closed during 1948. The remains of the facility have provided the vantage point for this image taken on 16th May 1966 as Stanier Class 5 no. 45297 approaches with a train of coal wagons. The engine was based at Crewe and would be condemned there in September 1967. Photograph by Bill Wright courtesy Michael Mercer.

Opposite CHATTERLEY – NO. D290

On 16th May 1966 English Electric Type 4 (Class 40) no. D290 passes Chatterley with what looks to be a train loaded with permanent way. New from Vulcan Foundry during August 1960, the locomotive was in service for just over 23 years before condemned. Photograph by Bill Wright courtesy Michael Mercer.

Above and opposite above COVENTRY STATION
Established by the London & Birmingham Railway in 1838, Coventry station was rebuilt and added to several times in the 19th and 20th centuries. For the West Coast Electrification scheme, the facility was completely replaced to the modernist designs of W.R. Headley and D. Shorten. The station was completed in May 1962 and these two images show the booking hall and platforms during September of that year. Both photographs by B.W.L. Brooksbank.

Opposite below COVENTRY STATION – NO. 41162 AND NO. 43011
Fowler 4P Class Compound 4-4-0 no. 41162 is face-to-face with Ivatt Class 4MT 2-6-0 no. 43011 at Coventry station in the 1950s. No. 41162 was based at Rugby for most of the decade, whilst no. 43011 spent time at Nuneaton before moving to Tebay in May 1957. From then, the locomotive was in the North West to withdrawal during February 1967. No. 41162 went to the scrap yard in June 1960. Photograph courtesy Rail-Online.

COVENTRY
1
2
3

41162
43011

Above COVENTRY STATION

After the 'Modernisation Plan', BR decided to create a luxury high speed train with a DMU formation. This was the 'Blue Pullman' and five sets were ordered from Metropolitan-Cammell Carriage & Wagon Co. in the late 1950s. All were in service by 1960 and distributed between the London Midland Region – two – and Western Region – three. As the electrification of the West Coast Main Line was instigated soon after, the LMR sets went to work on the Midland Main Line as the 'Midland Pullman'. This ran from St Pancras to Manchester Central with a schedule of 3 hours 15 minutes, reducing the previous fastest time by just over half-an-hour. After completion of the WCML electrification, the two sets were withdrawn to the WR and a new 'Manchester Pullman' offered, and some 45 minutes quicker between Euston and Manchester. A 'Blue Pullman' set has stopped at Coventry station with a special service in the 1960s. Photograph by Ray Reed courtesy Colour-Rail.

Opposite COVENTRY STATION – NO. E3093

After the announcement of the West Coast Electrification scheme, BR produced a list of specifications for locomotive builders to produce prototype electrics. The AL1 was built by Associated Electrical Industries and served as a basis for the subsequent AL5. This class of 40 locomotives was constructed by BR's Doncaster Works from 1961 to 1964. No. E3093 was a late example and entered traffic in November 1963. An unidentified class mate stands behind the locomotive at Coventry station on 5th May 1966. No. 3093 was in service to 1990. Photograph courtesy Rail-Online.

COVENTRY
E70635E
D5005
D5005
COVENTRY
COVENTRY

Above DILHORNE

In the early 1890s, a short branch was laid from the North Staffordshire Railway to Foxfield Colliery, Dilhorne. When the mine closed in the mid-1960s, a group stepped in to form a heritage line – the Foxfield Railway. W.G. Bagnall 0-6-0ST *Lewisham* was donated to the line in 1970. The locomotive had been built in 1927 for the Shropshire Beet Sugar Co., Alscott. Seen here in May 1971, *Lewisham*'s boiler certificate expired in 2007 and at present is stored at the Foxfield Railway awaiting an overhaul. Photograph by Bill Reed.

Opposite COVENTRY STATION – NO. D5005 AND NO. 45670

Sulzer Type 2 (Class 24) no. D5005 is with Stanier 'Jubilee' Class 4-6-0 no. 45670 *Howard of Effingham* at Coventry station in the early to mid-1960s. No. D5005 was an early class member built by Derby Works in January 1959 and, according to derbysulzers.com, a decade later became part of an identity swap with no. D5025. The latter was scrapped but no. D5005 was kept in traffic as the locomotive. This saw no. D5005 (as no. D5025) survive to 1976. No. 45670 had no reprieve when condemned during 1964. Photograph courtesy Rail-Online.

DUDLEY STATION – NO. 8742

Collett 5700 Class 0-6-0PT no. 8742 has a goods train at Dudley station in July 1957. Photograph by Les Hanson from the David Hanson Archive courtesy Rail-Online.

Above DUDLEY STATION – NO. 41226

An auto-train from Dudley Port arrives at Dudley station with Ivatt Class 2MT 2-6-2T no. 41226 on 24th March 1951. Photograph by B.W.L. Brooksbank.

Below DUDLEY STATION – NO. 49202

At Dudley station for shunting duties on 24th March 1951 is Cooke G1 Class 0-8-0 no. 49202. Photograph by B.W.L. Brooksbank.

42331
LOOK AND LISTEN

Above EVESHAM – NO. PWM650

Ruston & Hornsby had a long history of building engines and in the early 1930s started erecting diesel locomotives. In 1953, the company supplied a diesel-electric shunter to BR for departmental use by the Western Region. Numbered PWM650, the locomotive was joined by four similar vehicles in 1959. The five were classified 97/6 under TOPS and survived into the privatisation era. No. PWM650 became no. 97650 in 1979 and was withdrawn during 1987. Purchased by the City of Lincoln – the place of the engine's birth – no. 97650 was on static display for a time before taken by the Lincolnshire Wolds Railway. At present, the locomotive is said to be at the Heritage Shunters Trust, Rowsley. This image shows no. PWM650 in service at Evesham on 23rd June 1963. Photograph courtesy Colour-Rail.

Opposite EVESHAM MIDLAND STATION – NO. 42331

The Birmingham & Gloucester Railway passed a number of places east of the company's route. The Midland Railway oversaw a project to connect these in 1859 and the task was completed by 1868. The new line ran from Barnt Green to Redditch, Alcester, Evesham and Ashchurch. Evesham Midland station opened on 1st October 1864 and was built adjacent to the GWR station, which was on the Oxford, Worcester & Wolverhampton Railway line. Fowler 4P Class no. 42331 is arriving with a local train at Evesham Midland station in May 1958. Just five years later, the line between Redditch and Ashchurch was closed. Photograph courtesy Rail-Online.

Above FENNY COMPTON – NO. 44188

Joining the Barnt Green-Ashchurch Loop with the Bedford-Northampton line, the Stratford-upon-Avon & Midland Junction Railway was scheduled for closure in the mid-1960s. The Stephenson Locomotive Society commemorated the event with a rail tour on 24th April 1965. Fowler 4F Class 0-6-0 no. 44188 was one of the locomotives used and has the train at Fenny Compton. Photograph by Brian Stephenson courtesy Rail-Online.

Opposite above and below HANDSWORTH & SMETHWICK STATION – NO. 9768

On 24th September 1964, Collett 5700 Class 0-6-0PT no. 9768 has a pick-up freight from Handsworth Yards at Handsworth & Smethwick station. The locomotive was condemned at the end of the year. Both photographs by Revd J. David Benson courtesy A1 Steam Trust.

9768

1X00

Above HANDSWORTH – NO. 6955

An unfitted express freight passes Handsworth behind Collett 'Hall' Class 4-6-0 no. 6955 *Lydcott Hall* on 20th July 1964. In the background is the loop from the Birmingham to Wolverhampton route to the Grand Junction Railway line. Photograph by Richard Postill.

Opposite HANDSWORTH & SMETHWICK STATION – NO. D1036

Western Type 4 (Class 52) no. D1036 *Western Emperor* is with the Royal Train and travelling through Handsworth & Smethwick station on 24th May 1963. However, the Queen was not on board and the set was to meet her again at Wolverhampton Low Level. Her Majesty was visiting Birmingham in relation to developments taking place, such as the Bull Ring shopping centre and ring road. No. 1036 was amongst the 44 Western Type 4s erected by Crewe Works and entered service in August 1962. New to Plymouth Laira, by the end of the year, a move to Old Oak Common had occurred. The locomotive returned to Laira in 1966 and was condemned there a decade later. Photograph courtesy Rail-Online.

1Z50

Above HANDSWORTH WOOD
In the late 1880s, the LNWR built a short connection from the original Grand Junction Railway to the Stour Valley Line. This passed through Handsworth Wood and a station opened there before the turn of the century, but closed owing to falling passenger numbers in the Second World War. A Derby Lightweight DMU is passing the site of the station with a service to Birmingham via Walsall c. 1960. Photograph courtesy Rail-Online.

Opposite HANDSWORTH – NO. D0260
The Birmingham Railway Carriage & Wagon Company, Associated Electrical Industries and Sulzer joined together and produced a design that met the Type 4 power classification for BR. No. D0260 *Lion* was completed in 1962 and was tested on the Western and Eastern Regions. After just two years, the locomotive was withdrawn as BR decided to purchase large numbers of Brush Type 4s. Some of the components were reused but the remainder of the locomotive was scrapped. No. D0260 is passing Handsworth whilst on test during April 1962. Photograph courtesy Rail-Online.

HENLEY IN ARDEN
HE LEY IN ARDEN
HENLEY-IN-ARDEN
HENLEY-IN-ARDEN
BRITISH RAILWAYS

Above HENLEY-IN-ARDEN STATION

A large number of three-car DMUs were ordered from Derby in the late 1950s. Destined for the Western Region, these units were later Class 116. The ex-GWR lines around Birmingham saw the vehicles take over services and the sets were formed of Driving Motor Brake Second, Trailer Composite and Driving Motor Second. A Class 116 DMU is at Henley-in-Arden station during September 1969. Photograph by Rob Tibbits courtesy Colour-Rail.

Opposite HENLEY-IN-ARDEN STATION – NO. 8108

No. 8108 started life in Churchward's 3100 Class when built at Swindon in January 1906. Numbered 3133 at this time, the locomotive later became no. 5133 during November 1928. From September 1939, the engine became part of the 8100 Class when rebuilt and renumbered 8108. The locomotive has a service at Henley-in-Arden station in June 1957. A long-term servant at Tyseley shed, no. 8108 was sent for scrap in November 1960. Photograph courtesy Rail-Online.

Above HEREFORD STATION – NO. D7001 AND NO. D7028

Despite being just a few years old, the Beyer, Peacock & Co. Type 3s (Class 35) were deemed non-standard by the British Railways Board when evaluating the designs in service at the end of the 1960s. This was due to the hydraulic transmission being at odds with the other Regions which had electric. Between 1971 and 1975, the locomotives were withdrawn and amidst this process, the 'Hymek Swansong' rail tour was organised for 22nd September 1973. The train left Paddington for Bristol, then crossed the Severn and ran via Abergavenny to Hereford. From there, the party travelled to Worcester, Oxford and Didcot where a return was made to London. The rail tour is at Hereford here with no. D7001 and no. D7028. Photograph courtesy Rail-Online.

Opposite HEREFORD STATION – NO. 2287

In the late 19th century William Dean produced the 2301 Class 0-6-0 and 260 locomotives were built. By the 1920s, these were becoming life expired and Collett modernised the type with the 2251 Class. From 1930 to 1948, 120 of these 0-6-0s appeared from Swindon Works, including no. 2287 in January 1936. Though mainly intended for freight services, the engines served a mixed traffic role when required and no. 2287 has a train of passenger carriages at Hereford station on 16th July 1964. Based locally between February and November 1964, the locomotive moved on to Gloucester for six months before condemned. Photograph courtesy Rail-Online.

Above HILLMORTON – NO. D371

The London & Birmingham Railway missed Northampton when built as Robert Stephenson wanted to keep gradients at a minimum and reaching the town would have required the line rising at an uncomfortable level. In 1845, the Northampton & Peterborough Railway provided a connection to the West Coast Main Line, then during the 1870s, the LNWR decided to build a loop from Rugby to Roade. The first section from Rugby to Northampton was completed in 1881 and the second opened the following year. South of Rugby the line split at the village (later suburb) of Hillmorton and English Electric Type 4 no. D371 has an express there on 20th April 1962. The train is on the L&BR whilst the track in the background is the Northampton Loop. Both have electrification gantries. No. D371 was just less than six months old and working from Camden at this time. Photograph courtesy Rail-Online.

Opposite HILLMORTON – NO. 46110

For over 30 years, Fowler's 'Royal Scot' Class 4-6-0s were seen at the head of many expresses on ex-LMSR lines. The Class was a victim of the 'Modernisation Plan' and all were condemned between 1962 and 1965. No. 46110 *Grenadier Guardsman* became a class member when completed by the North British Locomotive Company in September 1927. The locomotive was part of the class-wide modernisation scheme and dealt with under BR in January 1953. This was just five years earlier when the engine was pictured with an express at Hillmorton during 1958. In that year no. 46110 moved several times and was at Camden, Kentish Town and Crewe North. Withdrawal from Carlisle Kingmoor occurred in February 1964. Photograph courtesy Colour-Rail.

6831

Above HONEYBOURNE – NO. 9620

The Oxford, Worcester & Wolverhampton Railway passed through the village of Honeybourne, five miles east of Evesham, when opened in 1853. At the end of the decade, a branch was built from just east of Honeybourne station to Stratford-upon-Avon and this later extended southwards to Cheltenham. The junction for these routes was important and sidings were installed nearby to stable trains for interchange. The West Yard and signal box are on the left here as Collett 8750 Class 0-6-0PT no. 9620 passes by with a short freight on 25th April 1964. This date was shortly before the end of freight at Honeybourne and passenger services had ceased in 1960. The station closed in 1969, though has been resurrected. Photograph by J.R. Newman courtesy Colour-Rail.

Opposite HONEYBOURNE – NO. 6831

A large number of Churchward 4300 Class 2-6-0s were in service by the 1930s, but at this time started to struggle with the assigned tasks, whilst also reaching around 20 years of age for the oldest examples. Collett decided to rebuild some class members as 6800 'Grange' Class 4-6-0s and 80 were dealt with at Swindon Works from 1936 to 1939 when the war stopped the project. No. 6831 *Bearley Grange* was built in August 1937. The locomotive has a freight service at Honeybourne on 25th April 1964. Allocated to Oxley, Wolverhampton, the engine was withdrawn there during October 1965. Photograph by J.R. Newman courtesy Colour-Rail.

48468

W 23 W

Above KIDDERMINSTER
Though usually in a three-car formation, this Class 120 DMU is just a pair at Kidderminster on 3rd August 1965. Built at Swindon Works in the late 1950s, 194 Class 120 vehicles entered service, mainly for the Western Region, though some went to Scotland. This two-car set is working a Worcester to Snow Hill service. Photograph courtesy Colour-Rail.

Opposite above KIDDERMINSTER – NO. 48468
To help with the movement of war materials, the Railway Executive Committee ordered a number of Stanier 8F 2-8-0s for use across Britain. Swindon Works built 80 examples between 1943 and 1945, including no. 48468 which appeared in March 1945. The locomotive has a coal train at Kidderminster on 27th February 1965. Based nearby at Stourbridge Junction, no. 48468 had been there since June 1964 and remained to July 1966 when transferred to Lostock Hall. After a year there, the engine moved to Burnley Rose Grove and was condemned in March 1968. Photograph courtesy Colour-Rail.

Opposite below KIDDERMINSTER STATION – NO. W23W
Kidderminster station opened with the Worcester to Stourbridge section of the Oxford, Worcester & Wolverhampton Railway. Dating from 1852, the first building did not survive past the end of the decade before replaced and the second structure lasted even less owing to fire. A Tudor-style station was erected in 1863 and used for over a century. On 12th June 1962, GWR railcar no. W23W is at Kidderminster station. Photograph by Bill Reed.

LAPWORTH
1V19

Above LAPWORTH STATION – NO. 5198

The Birmingham & Oxford Junction Railway was promoted by the GWR to gain an interest in traffic to the West Midlands. Completed in 1852, the line passed through the village of Kingswood, south east of Birmingham, and a station was provided there two years after opening. The facility was originally titled Kingswood but in the early 20th century this changed to Lapworth for the settlement to the west. Collett 5101 Class 2-6-2T no. 5198 has a train at the station in the late 1950s. Photograph courtesy Rail-Online.

Opposite LAPWORTH STATION – NO. D1746

Brush Type 4 (Class 47) no. D1746 was around a year old when caught with a Western Region express at Lapworth station during 1965. The locomotive was completed at Loughborough in July 1964 and first allocated to Old Oak Common shed. No. D1746 later worked for the London Midland Region and Eastern Region. Photograph courtesy Colour-Rail.

LEAMINGTON SPA STATION
The Western Region 'Blue Pullman' from Paddington to Wolverhampton is at Leamington Spa station. Photograph courtesy Colour-Rail.

Above LEAMINGTON SPA STATION – NO. 4149
Collett 5101 Class 2-6-2T no. 4149 has a short local train at Leamington Spa station during May 1961. The locomotive was condemned early in 1963. Photograph by Bill Reed.

Below LEAMINGTON SPA STATION – NO. 5912
A trio of young gentlemen engage the crew of Collett 'Hall' Class 4-6-0 no. 5912 *Queen's Hall* whilst the engine stands at Leamington Spa station in May 1961. Photograph by Bill Reed.

GENERAL
WAITING ROOM

4088

Above LEDBURY STATION – NO. W19W
On 27th June 1959, GWR railcar no. W19W has reached Ledbury with the 16.08 service from Gloucester. Photograph by L. Rowe courtesy Colour-Rail.

Opposite above LEDBURY STATION – NO. 4628
On the line of the Worcester & Hereford Railway, Ledbury station opened under the West Midland Railway in September 1861. Around this time, the GWR took over the Herefordshire & Gloucestershire Canal and part of the route became the basis for the Ledbury & Gloucester Railway. The line opened in July 1885. Collett 5700 Class 0-6-0PT no. 4628 has just worked a Gloucester to Ledbury train and is running to the other end for the return service on 8th November 1958. The last passenger train ran during the following year and freight ceased in 1964. No. 4628 was also condemned during the year. Photograph by B.W.L. Brooksbank.

Opposite below LEDBURY STATION – NO. 4088
A westbound express runs through Ledbury station with 'Castle' Class 4-6-0 no. 4088 *Dartmouth Castle* on 27th June 1959. The locomotive was Worcester-based at the time. Photograph courtesy Rail-Online.

Above LICHFIELD TRENT VALLEY STATION – NO. 46156

The line from Rugby to Stafford opened at Lichfield in 1847, then the South Staffordshire Railway crossed this route during 1849 when trains began travelling between Dudley and Burton-on-Trent. Both lines were later operated by the LNWR and the company built a joint station in 1871 with high-level and low-level platforms. 'Royal Scot' Class no. 46156 *The South Wales Borderer* is at the latter with a Manchester London Road to Euston service on 4th June 1962. Photograph by B.W.L. Brooksbank.

Opposite LICHFIELD – NO. DP1

English Electric Type 5 prototype no. DP1 *Deltic* is just north of Lichfield Trent Valley station at Netherstowe Lane with an express in 1956. The locomotive was tested on the London Midland Region from late 1955, then later settled to regular duties. These were between Crewe and Euston, as well as Liverpool and Euston. Early in 1959, no. DP1 started trials on the Eastern Region. Photograph courtesy Rail-Online.

Above LICKEY INCLINE – NO. D85

Though Isambard Kingdom Brunel surveyed a gentler route between Gloucester and Birmingham, this was longer and more expensive. A second survey tackled the Lickey Incline, between Bromsgrove and Blackwell, and was accepted through lower cost but the difficulty in ascending the bank (two miles at 1 in 37) was great, especially for the time. Opened in September 1840, the Lickey Incline was initially worked by two American locomotives before others were engaged. After the end of steam, these could be a pair of English Electric Type 3s (Class 37) or Beyer, Peacock & Co. Type 3s (Class 35). A Derby Type 4 (Class 45), no. D85 is with a train on the incline during the mid-1960s. Photograph courtesy Rail-Online.

Opposite above LICKEY INCLINE

The final development of the GWR 0-6-0PT was the Hawksworth 9400 Class. The first ten appeared under the company before Nationalisation, then another 200 locomotives were built by contractors up to the mid-1950s. A small group of class members was put to work on banking trains up Lickey Incline and two are assisting here on 5th September 1959. Photograph by Geoff Warnes.

Opposite below LICKEY INCLINE

A number of locomotive classes worked as bankers for trains ascending the Lickey Incline. Whilst the Midland Railway provided the dedicated 0-10-0 no. 2290 'Big Bertha', a selection of 3F 0-6-0Ts were also on hand for many years. From 1958, the jurisdiction of the area passed from the London Midland Region to the Western Region, which went on to employ 0-6-0PTs as well as a BR Standard Class 9F 2-10-0. A 3F Class and 9400 Class locomotive help a train on the bank in early September 1959. Photograph by Geoff Warnes.

Above LICKEY INCLINE
The Derby Type 4 (Class 45) was initially concentrated on the Midland Main Line, then started travelling further afield, such as to Newcastle and Bristol. When working from the latter back to the Midlands, the class had to tackle the Lickey Incline and a test was performed to determine the suitability of the design and possible banking requirements. On 20th September 1961, no. D40 was brought to a stop before the incline, then released with 16 carriages and was able to reach around 25 mph without assistance. An unidentified Derby Type 4 is travelling down the bank during May 1963. Photograph courtesy Rail-Online.

Opposite LICKEY INCLINE – NO. 92231
BR Standard Class 9F 2-10-0 no. 92231 was completed at Crewe Works in August 1958 and sent into service at Pontypool Road shed, Newport. The engine went on to be moved several times around South Wales and Bristol before starting again on the Southern Region where work was found at Eastleigh, then Feltham. After three years at York from September 1963 to November 1966, no. 92231 was condemned. The locomotive is pictured at the rear of a passenger train ascending the Lickey Incline on 29th August 1959. Photograph by Geoff Warnes.

Above LITTLETON COLLIERY

Manning Wardle (works no. 2018) 0-6-0ST no. 5 *Littleton* was one of two locomotives purchased from the company in 1922 for employment at Littleton Colliery, Cannock, Staffordshire. No. 5 was taken into preservation during 1972, first to Foxfield, then the Great Central Railway, Loughborough. Moving on in 1980, the locomotive found a home at the Avon Valley Railway and currently resides there awaiting overhaul. No. 5 is pictured still at work on the Littleton Colliery site during mid-May 1971. Photograph by Bill Reed.

Opposite above LITTLETON COLLIERY – NO. 6

In the mid-1950s, the Yorkshire Engine Co. developed the 'Janus' Class diesel-electric locomotive which had a central cab for shunting. More than 100 examples were built over the next few years, mainly for steel works around the country, but the National Coal Board also took seven locomotives. One of these was dispatched to Littleton Colliery and no. 6 is seen there on 17th May 1971. Subsequently taken into private industry, the locomotive was preserved in the late 2000s and went to the North Staffordshire Railway, being christened *Roger H. Bennett* after the benefactor who made the purchase possible. Photograph by Bill Reed.

Opposite below LITTLETON COLLIERY

Littleton Colliery was active from the 1870s to 1993 and the site has been redeveloped. Hunslet 0-6-0ST no. 4 *Robert Nelson* is working there on 7th May 1971. Photograph by Bill Reed.

ROBERT NELSON Nº4

MADELEY – NO. E3112
AL6 (Class 86) no. E3112 is with a test train at Madeley on 31st October 1971. Photograph courtesy Rail-Online.

Above MADELEY – NO. 46233

Stanier 'Coronation' Class Pacific no. 46233 *Duchess of Sutherland* passes Madeley with the 13.05 Euston to Perth service on 19th April 1962. Photograph by B.W.L. Brooksbank.

Below MADELEY – NO. 45288

At Madeley with a relief express bound for Euston is Stanier Class 5 4-6-0 no. 45288. Seen on 19th April 1962, the engine was based at Willesden. Photograph by B.W.L. Brooksbank.

MUCH WENLOCK
B2

Above MUCH WENLOCK STATION – NO. 5167

Several undertakings were necessary to link Buildwas, near Telford, and Craven Arms. Much Wenlock station was originally a terminus for the Much Wenlock & Severn Junction Railway when opened in February 1862. The Wenlock, Craven Arms & Lightmoor Extension connected Lightmoor with Buildwas, then Much Wenlock to Craven Arms. For this, Much Wenlock station moved a short distance and reopened in April 1866, being used for just under a century. The passenger services to Craven Arms were withdrawn in 1951 and those between Wellington and Much Wenlock followed during 1962. Collett 5101 Class 2-6-2T no. 5167 is at Much Wenlock station in August 1959. Photograph by F. Hornby courtesy Colour-Rail.

Opposite MUCH WENLOCK STATION

Gloucester Railway Carriage & Wagon Co. DMU (Class 122), no. W55009, has a train for Wellington at Much Wenlock station on 14th July 1962. The unit was part of the group built by the company to replace the original GWR railcars. No. W55009 was sent into service at Tyseley during May 1958 and withdrawn in 1993. Subsequently preserved, the unit is at the Great Central Railway awaiting restoration. Photograph courtesy Rail-Online.

NUNEATON TRENT VALLEY STATION – NO. E3064

AL5 (Class 85) no. E3064 is light engine at Nuneaton Trent Valley station during the early 1960s. Photograph courtesy Rail-Online.

Above NUNEATON TRENT VALLEY STATION – NO. 46166
In the early 1960s, 'Royal Scot' Class no. 46166 *London Rifle Brigade* makes a stop at Nuneaton Trent Valley station. Photograph by Bill Reed.

Below NUNEATON TRENT VALLEY STATION – NO. D7659
Sulzer Type 2 (Class 25) no. D7659 stands at Nuneaton Trent Valley station during 1966. An English Electric Type 4 (Class 40) is seen on the right. Photograph courtesy Rail-Online.

S·L·S SPECIAL
17802

Above OSWESTRY – NO. 1458

In the early 20th century, the GWR sought to improve the operation of branch line services and introduced a number of autocoaches and autotrains. These had controls in one end of the carriage which stopped the need for the driver to be on the footplate, as well as the locomotive having to run around the coach. The GWR built autocoaches for 50 years and completed 241 examples. Collett designed the 4800 Class (later 1400 Class) 0-4-2T locomotive to be used on the services in the early 1930s and 75 examples were constructed. No. 1458 (originally no. 4858) was produced at Swindon in August 1935. The locomotive is coupled to the rear end of an autotrain led by coach no. W225W on 7th April 1963 and the set is pictured at Oswestry. Photograph courtesy Rail-Online.

Opposite OSWESTRY STATION – NO. 7802

The Stephenson Locomotive Society's 'Farewell to the Cambrian Railways' was postponed twice before running on 17th January 1965. The original date was 22nd November 1964, though this was pushed back to 3rd January 1965 and in the meantime, the section of the route between Ruabon and Morfa Mawddach (previously Barmouth Junction) was flooded. This saw the tour rerouted to view the Llanfyllin branch instead. Collett 'Manor' Class 4-6-0 no. 7802 *Bradley Manor* started the day at Shrewsbury and travelled to Welshpool, Oswestry and Whitchurch where Ivatt Class 2MT no. 46512 took over for Llanfyllin. Returning northwards to Gobowen, no. 7802 was recoupled to the train and finished the tour at Shrewsbury. The locomotive is at Oswestry here. Photograph by Richard Postill.

6916

Above OXLEY SHED – NO. D1007

Extensive sidings were located alongside the GWR's line from Wolverhampton to Wellington. An engine shed was installed there in 1907 and consisted of two roundhouses joined together. These were in use for 60 years, then being demolished. Western Region Type 4 (Class 52) no. D1007 *Western Talisman* is seen outside during 1962. New from Swindon Works in August of that year, the locomotive had all-over maroon livery, but soon after acquired a small yellow warning panel at the ends. No. D1007 had a career lasting just less than 12 years. Photograph courtesy Rail-Online.

Opposite OXLEY – NO. 6906

Just north of Bushbury Junction at Oxley, Collett 'Hall' Class 4-6-0 no. 6906 *Chicheley Hall* has a train of mineral wagons on 22nd June 1963. This was the point where the Stour Valley Line rejoined the Grand Junction Railway. No. 6906 was built at Swindon in November 1940 and ran to April 1965. Photograph by Richard Postill.

4135

Above POLESWORTH – NO. 45634

East of Tamworth at Polesworth, Stanier 'Jubilee' Class 4-6-0 no. 45634 *Trinidad* has a train featuring cattle wagons and containers. Pictured on 3rd June 1955, the locomotive was in the middle of an allocation to Crewe North which lasted from the start of the year to December when a transfer to Bushbury occurred. Photograph by Bill Reed.

Opposite ROSS-ON-WYE STATION – NO. 4135

Ross-on-Wye station opened with the Hereford, Ross & Gloucester Railway on 1st June 1855. A new line from Monmouth reached Ross-on-Wye during 1873. The latter was the first to close in 1959, then the Hereford to Gloucester route followed during the mid-1960s. Collett 5101 Class 2-6-2T no. 4135 has the 16.08 Gloucester to Hereford at Ross-on-Wye in May 1962. The engine had recently moved to Hereford shed and was condemned there two years later. Photograph by Tony Cooke courtesy Colour-Rail.

Above RUGBY STATION – NO. D212

The 08.30 Carlisle and Windemere train to Euston has reached Rugby station with English Electric Type 4 (Class 40) no. D212 on 30th October 1959. The locomotive had been completed by Vulcan Foundry in May 1959 and allocated to Willesden, though moved on to Crewe North, then reached Carlisle during September. Allocated there for just over a year, no. D212 spent the first half of the 1960s at Camden shed. Before leaving Carlisle, the locomotive became one of the few English Electric Type 4s to be named and also part of an even smaller group that had an official ceremony. No. D212 was christened *Aureol* after an ocean liner operated by Elder Dempster Lines. The locomotive was in traffic to 1986 and has been preserved. Photograph by B.W.L. Brooksbank.

Opposite RUGBY CLIFTON ROAD – NO. D5074

To the east of Rugby, the Northampton Loop (carried by the brick arches) branched off from the West Coast Main Line, whilst the Rugby & Stamford Railway curved away to the north east. Sulzer Type 2 (Class 24) no. D5074 approaches on the Northampton route with a passenger service, whilst a Stanier Class 5 4-6-0 is travelling from Stamford with a freight train during the early 1960s. No. D5074 was new to March shed in March 1960 but moved to London in the following month. Photograph by Bill Reed.

RUGBY CLIFTON ROAD – NO. 46245

Stanier 'Coronation' Class Pacific no. 46245 *City of London* has an express at Rugby Clifton Road, c. 1960. Photograph by Bill Reed.

RUGBY CLIFTON ROAD – NO. D219

Approaching Rugby with an express, c. 1960, is English electric Type 4 (Class 40) no. D219. Photograph by Bill Reed.

45705
45705

49342

Above RUGBY STATION – NO. DP1

A young gentleman looks into the engine room of English Electric Type 5 no. DP1 *Deltic*, which has stopped at Rugby with a London-bound express on 15th February 1958. The locomotive was powered by two Napier Deltic units which produced 3,300 horsepower. Photograph courtesy Rail-Online.

Opposite above RUGBY SHED – NO. 45705

Blackpool-allocated Stanier 'Jubilee' no. 45705 *Seahorse* is at Rugby shed c. 1960. The locomotive was in the North West from June 1956 to June 1964. No. 45705 had around 18 months at Newton Heath afterwards before condemned. Photograph by Bill Reed.

Opposite below RUGBY SHED – NO. 49342

Following on from the A Class, Webb's B Class 0-8-0 experimented with four compound cylinders. The design was built from 1901 to 1904 and numbered 170 examples. The B Class also proved a disappointment and many were reconstructed subsequently. No. 49342 was originally part of the class when produced at Crewe during October 1902. C.B. Cooke transformed a number to the G1 Class with two cylinders and a superheated boiler. The engine joined this group in December 1919 and was further upgraded to G2A in October 1935. No. 49342 is seen near Rugby shed, c. 1960. With '2B' on the smokebox door, the locomotive was allocated to Nuneaton and this lasted from November 1952 to October 1961 when withdrawn. In the background on the right is Rugby Testing Station. Photograph by Bill Reed.

44057

Above SALTLEY SHED – NO. D7602

In the early 1850s, the MR developed locomotive servicing facilities at Saltley. These evolved over the years and at the turn of the century consisted of three roundhouses. Following the 'Modernisation Plan' BR replaced these with a diesel depot which survived until 2000. The site is still occupied by the railways. This image dates from February 1966 and features a line of diesel locomotives headed by Sulzer Type 2 (Class 25) no. D7602 which was based at Tinsley. Photograph by R. Mabey courtesy Colour-Rail.

Opposite above SALTLEY STATION – NO. 44057

View northwards at Saltley station on 22nd April 1965 as Fowler 4F Class 0-6-0 no. 44057 travels tender-first on the up goods line. The Birmingham & Derby Junction Railway created the route between the two places in 1840, connecting the North Midland Railway and London & Birmingham Railway. Saltley station was not built until 1854 and underwent reconstruction at the end of the century. Only three years remained for the facility before closure. The local area had a number of railway establishments, such as Saltley locomotive shed, which was to the south, in addition to Lawley Street Goods station and sidings. Just off to the north east – and visible here on the right – were the Metropolitan Cammell carriage works, whilst the company had a second site a short distance away at Washwood Heath. Also there was the ex-Midland Railway marshalling yard. Photograph by B.W.L. Brooksbank.

Opposite below SALTLEY SHED – NO. 4139

Fowler 4F Class 0-6-0 no. 4139 was erected at Crewe Works in October 1925. The locomotive is seen at Saltley shed on 30th March 1946. The BR number was applied from July 1949. Withdrawal occurred in August 1965. Photograph by B.W.L. Brooksbank.

42400

45406

Above SHREWSBURY STATION – NO. D1740 AND NO. D1726

As part of the diesel switchover, BR identified the need for a large number of Type 4 locomotives with a 19-ton axle load. The trade offered several designs and the one chosen was from Brush Traction, Loughborough. Twenty were ordered initially before five more batches followed and the class (TOPS 47) totalled 512 examples. No. D1740 and no. D1726 were part of a group ordered in September 1962 and built in June and March 1964 respectively. The two locomotives are at Shrewsbury station on 22nd June 1964. Photograph by David Christie.

Opposite above SHREWSBURY STATION – NO. 42400

From 1927 to 1934, 125 of Fowler's 4P Class 2-6-4T locomotives were built at Derby Works. No. 42400 was amongst the group when completed there in September 1933. By this time, a small change was made to the design as windows were provided for the cab instead of the old-style cutouts. This affected 30 4Ps. No. 42400 is at Shrewsbury station on 22nd June 1964. Allocated to Stafford, withdrawal from there took place in late January 1965. Photograph by David Christie.

Opposite below SHREWSBURY STATION – NO. 45406

Stanier Class 5 no. 45406 was a long-term resident at Shrewsbury shed and is backing out of the station to return there on 22nd June 1964. The locomotive left for Annesley in October and had a year there before moving to Kirkby-in-Ashfield. Colwick and Speke Junction had the services of no. 45406 for a year and six months respectively before the engine was condemned in July 1967. Photograph by David Christie.

0000

Above SHREWSBURY STATION – NO. 4153 AND NO. 6934
Collett 5101 Class 2-6-2T no. 4153 has a mineral train at Shrewsbury station on 23rd February 1963, whilst Collett 'Hall' Class 4-6-0 no. 6934 *Beachamwell Hall* stands against the platform with a passenger service. No. 4153 held a long-term allocation to Kidderminster shed and no. 6934 worked locally. Photograph by Richard Postill.

Opposite SHREWSBURY – NO. D0260
Early in 1962 the Birmingham Railway Carriage & Wagon Co. prototype diesel locomotive no. D0260 *Lion* reached completion. During April, several test runs from Smethwick to Shrewsbury and Banbury were carried out and one with the headcode of 0O00 was recorded as taking place on 21st April. The locomotive is at Shrewsbury here and likely on that date. The image shows the striking livery of white, whilst the sides were accented with gold lines. The buffer beam was later painted black. On 6th May, no. D0260 was presented to the British Transport Commission at Marylebone station, then began trials on 14th May. Photograph courtesy Colour-Rail.

SOLIHULL
5194

Above SOLIHULL – NO. D1038

The Western Region Type 4 (Class 52) was designed in response to increasing train loads which could not be met by existing Type 2s and Type 3s except when working together. Two Maybach MD655 V12 engines were fitted and these produced 1,350 horsepower each at 1,500 rpm, whilst the hydraulic transmission was a Voith L630 unit. In service, these were found to be unsuitable together through the gearing and this contributed to the early withdrawal of the class. One member, no. D1038 *Western Sovereign*, has an express at Solihull during April 1963. The locomotive was just over six months old and working from Old Oak Common, yet in May 1963 a transfer to Cardiff occurred. Photograph by M. Mensing courtesy Colour-Rail.

Opposite SOLIHULL STATION – NO. 5194

The Oxford & Rugby Railway was promoted to connect with the early rail centre at Rugby where several important lines met. After authorisation and before work started, the GWR stepped in and took over. Instead of reaching Rugby, the GWR saw the line as a stepping stone in their endeavour to have a portion of the traffic to Birmingham and beyond. An extension from the O&RR north of Fenny Compton was authorised in 1846 as the Birmingham & Oxford Junction Railway. The two sections opened in 1850 and 1852 respectively and Solihull station was completed during the latter year. This survived to the 1930s when track improvements saw the buildings demolished and resited to the south. Further modifications were carried out after the end of steam owing to reduced use of the lines, though these remain an important alternative to the WCML. Collett 5101 Class 2-6-2T no. 5194 has a local train at Solihull station in the late 1950s. Photograph courtesy Rail-Online.

1A33
E3018

Above STAFFORD STATION – NO. 46150

By the mid-1920s, the LMSR needed a suitable express locomotive. The Board of the company obtained a Collett 'Castle' Class locomotive on loan from the GWR and after trials a new 4-6-0 was proposed. The Fowler 'Royal Scot' Class was built by the North British Locomotive Company in 1927 (50 engines) and Derby Works during 1930 (20). No. 46150 *The Life Guardsman* was the first 'Royal Scot' erected at Derby in June 1930. The locomotive is at Stafford station with the 09.10 from Llandudno to Euston on 14th April 1960. Photograph by B.W.L. Brooksbank.

Opposite STAFFORD STATION – NO. E3018

The Grand Junction Railway opened the first station at Stafford on 4th July 1837. This was on the line from Birmingham to Warrington where a connection with the Liverpool & Manchester Railway was made. Stafford's station has been replaced several times, with the present facility dating from 1962 and to the design of W.R. Headley. The station was built as part of the West Coast Electrification Scheme and one of the prototype electric locomotives is at Stafford on 26th June 1964. AL1 (Class 81) no. E3018 was one of 25 class members built by Associated Electrical Industries and entered service in March 1961. Photograph by David Christie.

D 5081

46508

Above STOKE-ON-TRENT STATION – NO. 44766
View northwards at Stoke-on-Trent station as Stanier Class 5 no. 44766 approaches with an unfitted express freight. On the left is the extensive goods yard, which was adjacent to the Trent & Mersey Canal, and has now been converted into the car park for the station. Stoke-on-Trent was opened by the North Staffordshire Railway in 1848 and has subsequently achieved Grade II listed status. No. 44766 has been pictured on 4th May 1965 and was working from Bescot at the time. Photograph by B.W.L. Brooksbank.

Opposite above STOKE-ON-TRENT – NO. D5081
The Staffordshire pottery towns of Burslem, Fenton, Hanley, Longton, Stoke-on-Trent and Tunstall amalgamated into the county borough of Stoke-on-Trent in 1910. As part of celebrations for the 50th anniversary of the event an exhibition of locomotives was arranged. One participant was recently constructed Sulzer Type 2 (Class 24) no. D5081. In service for 20 years, the locomotive was the final class member withdrawn and became one of four Class 24s to be preserved. Working on the Gloucestershire Warwickshire Railway, no. D5081 is presently active. Photograph by Bill Reed.

Opposite below STOKE-ON-TRENT SHED – NO. 46508
Contrasting with the work-worn engines behind, Ivatt Class 2MT 2-6-0 no. 46508 gleams in the yard at Stoke-on-Trent shed early in April 1963. The locomotive had been a visitor to Crewe Works for attention and would return to service at Croes Newydd. No. 46508 had been allocated there for just two months and this lasted two years. Withdrawal from Shrewsbury occurred in December 1966. Visible in the background is Stanier Class 5 no. 44679. Photograph courtesy Rail-Online.

Above STOURBRIDGE JUNCTION STATION – NO. 4146
The Oxford, Worcester & Wolverhampton Railway passed near to Stourbridge and opened a station for the town in 1852. An independent company later extended from Stourbridge to make a junction with the Stour Valley Line near Smethwick and the route was completed at the end of the 1860s. Further developments were carried out in the late 1870s as the GWR decided to open a branch to the town and this one-mile link was ready in 1879/1880. A new station at Stourbridge to better serve the junctions was built at the turn of the century. Circa 1960, Collett 5101 Class 2-6-2T no. 4146 is light engine at Stourbridge, whilst a Class 116 DMU has a service for Bewdley. Photograph courtesy Rail-Online.

Opposite STOURBRIDGE JUNCTION STATION – NO. 1011
F.W. Hawksworth became CME of the GWR in 1941 and due to the war had time to think about future traffic requirements, as well as new locomotive features to meet them. Starting with the 'Modified Hall' Class 4-6-0, he also produced the 'County' Class 4-6-0 for mixed traffic duties between 1945 and 1947, numbering 30 examples. No. 1011 *County of Chester* was amongst these and completed at Swindon in January 1946. The class worked around the Western Region for 15 years before withdrawals started and proceeded relatively rapidly from 1962 to 1964 when becoming extinct. Just before this, the Stephenson Locomotive Society's Midland Branch was able to run a commemorative rail tour on 20th September 1964. No. 1011 *County of Chester* was the last 'County' in service and used for the day. Starting at Snow Hill, Birmingham, the locomotive travelled to Swindon via Gloucester, then returned using the Oxford route. No. 1011 is seen during a stop at Stourbridge Junction on the outward leg. The locomotive was withdrawn in November 1964. A new-build 'County' Class locomotive is presently being constructed. Photograph by Richard Postill.

STRATFORD-UPON-AVON STATION

A Class 116 DMU arrives at Stratford-upon-Avon station during April 1960. Photograph courtesy Colour-Rail.

Above STRATFORD-UPON-AVON STATION – NO. 4614

A local train has just taken water at Stratford-upon-Avon station during April 1960. The locomotive is Collett 8750 Class 0-6-0PT no. 4614. Photograph courtesy Colour-Rail.

Below STRATFORD-UPON-AVON STATION – NO. 44777

Stanier Class 5 no. 44777 has also made a stop for water at Stratford-upon-Avon station, c. 1960. The locomotive was in service almost to the end of steam. Photograph by R. Mabey courtesy Colour-Rail.

Above TAMWORTH – NO. D115

Near Tamworth with an express on 8th February 1967 is Derby Type 4 (Class 45) no. D115. The locomotive was built at Crewe Works in August 1961 and went on to have the distinction of being the first Class 45 withdrawn in July 1977. This was due to a collision near Ilkeston on 8th July as no. D115, then renumbered 45067, ran into a coal wagon which had derailed. No fatalities occurred and the locomotive was stored at Derby Works for three years before finally scrapped in June 1980. Photograph courtesy Rail-Online.

Opposite TAMWORTH – NO. 48681

Before the advent of the 'Austerity' Class 2-8-0, the Stanier Class 8F was chosen by the War Department as the standard freight design for use in conflict zones. The 8F was also built in numbers for the Railway Executive Committee which oversaw the 'Big Four' during the Second World War. From 1943 to 1945, 245 were built at several locations, including the Southern Railway's Brighton Works. Sixty-eight locomotives were erected there in 1943 and 1944, including no. 48681, which is at Tamworth with a train of coal wagons on 22nd August 1965. Completed in January 1944, the engine was later a long-term servant at Toton shed, though by the time of the image a transfer had recently occurred where Burton held the allocation. No. 48681 was withdrawn in July 1967 after several months at Northwich. Photograph by Bill Wright courtesy Michael Mercer.

Above TYSELEY SHED – NO. 7029

At the end of steam, Tyseley shed became the home of the privately purchased 'Castle' Class 4-6-0 no. 7029 *Clun Castle* and has subsequently grown to stable other locomotives. On 29th and 30th September 1968, the first open days were held and no. 7029 has been pictured then. Photograph by Bill Reed.

Below TYSELEY SHED – NO. 4555

Churchward 4500 Class 2-6-2T no. 4555 was bought for preservation in 1964 and later went to work on the Dart Valley Railway, subsequently renamed the South Devon Railway. The engine was stored at Tyseley in the meantime and sits inside the shed on 22nd November 1964. Photograph by Bill Reed.

Above TYSELEY SHED – NO. 48773 AND NO. W22W

Stanier 8F no. 48773 was saved from the scrapyard by the Stanier 8F Locomotive Society and subsequently found a home at the Severn Valley Railway. The latter also accommodated GWR railcar no. W22W which was bought from BR in 1967 and is now based at the Didcot Railway Centre. The two are at Tyseley on 29th September 1968. Photograph by Geoff Warnes.

Below TYSELEY SHED – NO. 5593

Withdrawn in October 1967, Stanier 'Jubilee' Class no. 45593 *Kolhapur* was purchased in early 1968 and restored to LMSR livery. The locomotive is at Tyseley on 29th September 1968. Photograph by Geoff Warnes.

13192

Above TYSELEY SHED – NO. D1685 AND NO. D1698

Tyseley shed was built by the GWR in 1908 and contained two turntables with radiating roads, as well as a repair shop and associated facilities. The allocation consisted of around 100 passenger and freight engines up to the 1960s when withdrawals began and closure to steam occurred in 1966. By this time, the site had switched over to DMU stabling and diesel locomotive servicing, with the repair shop demolished and a new building for diesel maintenance erected. Two Brush Type 4s (Class 47) are at Tyseley in 1965. On the left is no. D1685, which was new to Oxley in November 1963, and to the right stands no. D1698 of Cardiff Canton depot. Photograph by R. Mabey courtesy Colour-Rail.

Opposite TYSELEY SHED – NO. 13192

In the early 1930s, the LMSR ordered nine prototype diesel shunters, with one supplied by Hawthorn Leslie which was based on an English Electric design. This was accepted by the LMSR and went into production for another ten examples. These served as the basis for 120 more shunters built between 1945 and 1952 (TOPS Class 11), then BR chose the type for use across the country (Class 08) and 996 were erected over a decade from 1952. No. 13192 was part of the group and emerged from Derby Works in November 1955, being allocated to Shrewsbury. Yet, the locomotive moved on to Tyseley a month later and is pictured at the shed on 27th May 1956. Leaving after five years, no. 13192, later no. D3192 and no. 08125, had a career lasting to 1981. Photograph by F. Hornby courtesy Colour-Rail.

UTTOXETER STATION – NO. 42663

Stanier 4P Class 2-6-4T no. 42663 has a local train at Uttoxeter station c. 1960. Photograph by Bill Reed.

Above UTTOXETER SHED – NO. 40653
In 1933, two Fowler 2P Class 4-4-0s were fitted with a Dabeg feedwater heater. No. 40653 was one of these engines and the apparatus is on the running plate next to the smokebox. Pictured out of service at Uttoxeter shed c. 1960, the locomotive was withdrawn during November 1959. Photograph by Bill Reed.

Below UTTOXETER SHED – NO. 40655
Another Fowler 4P 4-4-0 being stored at Uttoxeter shed was no. 40655. Both were allocated to Crewe shed during their final two years in service. Photograph by Bill Reed.

Above WASHWOOD HEATH – NO. 92029

A freight service departs from Washwood Heath goods sidings during the 1960s, with BR Standard Class 9F no. 92029 leading the wagons. The bridge in the background carries the Aston to Stechford line. Photograph courtesy Rail-Online.

Below WASHWOOD HEATH – NO. D2

Derby Type 4 (Class 44) no. D2 *Helvellyn* travels light engine at Washwood Heath during 1965. Photograph by R. Mabey courtesy Colour-Rail.

Above WEDNESBURY
The South Staffordshire Railway was the first to pass through Wednesbury as the company connected Dudley with Burton-on-Trent. A station opened there in 1850 and just four years later a second facility was built as the GWR created a route from Birmingham to Wolverhampton. This Class 116 DMU is running on the latter and travelling towards Wednesbury Central station during the 1960s with a Snow Hill to Wellington service. Until 1950, the station had been known as Wednesbury and the SSR stop changed to Wednesbury Town. The latter was closed in 1964, whilst Central survived into the 1970s, though has since been resurrected as part of the West Midlands Metro. Photograph courtesy Rail-Online.

Opposite WEDNESBURY – NO. 4094
Collett introduced the 4073 or 'Castle' Class 4-6-0 shortly after taking the position of Chief Mechanical Engineer of the GWR in 1922. His design was based on Churchward's 'Star' Class 4-6-0 and modernised to meet new demands on long-distance expresses. The first, no. 4073 *Caerphilly Castle*, appeared in 1923 and a steady stream of locomotives left Swindon up to 1950, totalling 155 examples, whilst 16 engines were rebuilt to 'Castle' specifications. No. 4094 *Dynevor Castle* was an early example and built in June 1926 as part of the third batch ordered. Around this time, Collett introduced the 4,000-gallon tender, but no. 4094 was sent into traffic with a Churchward-type 3,500-gallon tender. A switch to the new design was necessary for the 'Castles' and from 1929, no. 4094 had the higher capacity tender. Later, under Hawksworth, 4,000-gallon tenders had straight sides – not stepped-out as Collett's – and these could be found behind 'Castle' locomotives. *Dynevor Castle* was the recipient in an exchange that occurred in late 1952 but this lasted only 18 months before a return to the Collett-type. For the last two years in service – starting in 1960 – no. 4094 was again with a Hawksworth tender. The locomotive has an express at Wednesbury in the mid- to late 1950s. Photograph courtesy Rail-Online.

WELLINGTON STATION – NO. D1733

In April 1964, Brush Type 4 (Class 47) no. D1733 was given an experimental livery of pale blue and the new BR corporate logo on the cab sides with a red background. This was done to augment a new carriage set with fresh livery. This train is not featured here, as no. D1733 works a regular service at Wellington station during June 1964. Photograph by David Christie.

Above WELLINGTON STATION – NO. 9472

Hawksworth 9400 Class 0-6-0PT no. 9472 has been caught at Wellington station on 12th June 1962. Allocated to Shrewsbury at this time, the locomotive moved to Barry at the end of the year. Photograph by Bill Reed.

Below WELLINGTON STATION – NO. 6007

Also at Wellington station on 12th June 1962 is Collett 'King' Class 4-6-0 no. 6007 *King William III*. The locomotive, which was a replacement for one damaged in an accident, had six months left in service. Photograph by Bill Reed.

No8

Above WEST CANNOCK COLLIERY

A long-term servant for West Cannock Colliery (near Hednesford), 0-6-0ST locomotive *Topham* was ordered from W.G. Bagnall & Co. in 1922 for work at the mine. During 1970, the engine was taken out of service and is awaiting a decision for the future on site during May 1971. In the following year, a preservation scheme was successful and *Topham* was in steam from 1973 to 1990. Located on the Spa Valley Railway now, the engine requires a restoration. Photograph by Bill Reed.

Opposite above WEST CANNOCK COLLIERY – NCB NO. 4

Hunslet 'Austerity' Class 0-6-0ST locomotive NCB no. 4 is under cover at West Cannock Colliery on 17th May 1971. Photograph by Bill Reed.

Opposite below WEST CANNOCK COLLIERY – NCB NO. 8

NCB no. 8 appears to be receiving attention at West Cannock Colliery during May 1971. Photograph by Bill Reed.

4602

Above WOLVERHAMPTON STATION
Wolverhampton High Level station was rebuilt for the West Coast Electrification Scheme and caused the closure of Wolverhampton Low Level, which was on the Paddington to Birkenhead route. A Class 101 DMU is at Wolverhampton station with a service to Chester, c. 1970. The unit is in BR blue livery with corporate logo and small yellow panel on the front end which was a variation used by the class from the late 1960s, though more had a full yellow face. Photograph courtesy Colour-Rail.

Opposite above WOLVERHAMPTON – NO. 4602
The GWR started using pannier tanks around the turn of the century owing to a greater suitability when using a Belpaire firebox, lower centre of gravity and allowing motion components, etc, to be accessed. After Grouping, the GWR was in need of an improved tank locomotive fleet and during 1929 Collett introduced the 5700 Class 0-6-0PT design. Although variations in features existed, 863 locomotives were erected to 1950 and could be found across the GWR system on freight duties, as well as short passenger movements. No. 4602 was built at Swindon Works in October 1941 and fell into the 8750 sub-class. The locomotive is seen working a goods train at Wolverhampton during June 1964. Withdrawal took place at the end of the year. Photograph by David Christie.

Opposite below WOLVERHAMPTON – NO. 4165
Shunting goods wagons at Wolverhampton on 22nd June 1964 is Collett 5101 Class 2-6-2T no. 4165. Following a break in construction due to the Second World War, new 5101 Class engines were built at Swindon Works in 1946 and continued to 1949. Forty locomotives appeared in this period and took the class total to 140. No. 4165 was a late addition, being completed in October 1948. Working from Oxley when pictured, no. 4165 was condemned there in October 1965. Photograph by David Christie.

1001

Above WORCESTER SHRUB HILL STATION – NO. 4680
A local service approaches Worcester Shrub Hill station with Collett 8750 Class 0-6-0PT no. 4680 on 13th July 1963. The locomotive was based locally from August 1957 to December 1965 when condemned. Photograph by Richard Postill.

Opposite WOLVERHAMPTON LOW LEVEL STATION – NO. 1000
The first Hawksworth 'County' Class 4-6-0 was no. 1000 *County of Middlesex* which entered service from Swindon Works in August 1945. The locomotive is pictured at Wolverhampton Low Level station on 13th June 1964 and this was only a few weeks before condemned at Swindon shed, where no. 1000 had been allocated at the start of the year. Photograph by Richard Postill.

Above WORCESTER SHRUB HILL STATION – NO. 5056

Though the 'Castle' Class 4-6-0 was widely regarded for excellent performance, Hawksworth was able to improve the steam circuit. This was done through changes to the superheater – an increase in the number of elements – and fitting a double chimney, which increased the area for the exhaust to escape. No. 5056 *Earl of Powis* was amongst the group of 'Castles' altered and the modifications were both made in November 1960. Pictured at Worcester Shrub Hill station on 16th April 1963, the locomotive survived for another year before condemned. Photograph by Bill Reed.

Opposite above WORCESTER SHED – NO. W33W

Despite the outbreak of war, the GWR was able to complete a number of railcars between 1940 and 1942. Most were single units, but there were two pairs of twins built at the end of the run. When one of these was destroyed by fire in 1949, the car was replaced by no. W33W, being paired with no. W38W. The set was also able to run with a trailer carriage forming a triplet. No. W33W is seen at Worcester shed on 22nd April 1962. Photograph by Bill Reed.

Opposite below WORCESTER SHRUB HILL STATION – NO. 4079 AND NO. D1661

To say goodbye to steam at Paddington station, the Locomotive Club of Great Britain arranged the 'Paddington Steam Farewell Rail Tour' on 20th November 1965. Recently preserved 'Castle' Class no. 4079 *Pendennis Castle* was used for the train which went to Worcester before returning to London. The locomotive is seen here at Shrub Hill station with Brush Type 4 (Class 47) no. D1661 *North Star* (now preserved) and a Class 116 DMU. Photograph by Richard Postill.

W 33 W

GREAT WESTERN
D 1661

BIBLIOGRAPHY

Allen, C.J. *Titled Trains of Great Britain*. 1983.
Christiansen, Rex. *A Region History of the Railways of Great Britain: Volume 7 West Midlands*. 1983.
Clough, David N. *British Rail Standard Diesels of the 1960s*. 2009.
Griffiths, Roger and Paul Smith. *The Directory of British Engine Sheds and Principal Locomotive Servicing Points: 1 Southern England, the Midlands, East Anglia and Wales*. 1999.
Haresnape, Brian. *Fowler Locomotives*. 1997.
Haresnape, Brian. *Stanier Locomotives*. 1974.
Hawkins, Chris and George Reeve. *LMS Engine Sheds: Volume Two The Midland Railway*. 1981.
Hooper, J. *The WD Austerity 2-8-0 – The BR Record*. 2010.
Hunt, David, John Jennison, Fred James and Bob Essery. *LMS Locomotive Profiles: No. 5 – The Mixed Traffic Class 5s Nos 5000-5224*. 2003.
Hunt, David, John Jennison, Fred James and Bob Essery. *LMS Locomotive Profiles: No. 6 – The Mixed Traffic Class 5s Nos 5225-5499 and 4658-4999*. 2004.
Hunt, David, John Jennison, Fred James and Bob Essery. *LMS Locomotive Profiles: No. 7 – The Mixed Traffic Class 5s Caprotti Valve Gear Engines and Class Summary*. 2006.
Hunt, David, John Jennison, Fred James and Bob Essery. *LMS Locomotive Profiles: No. 8 – The Class 8F 2-8-0s*. 2005.
Hunt, David, John Jennison, Bob Essery and Fred James. *LMS Locomotive Profiles: No. 10 – The Standard Class 4 Goods 0-6-0s*. 2007.
Longworth, Hugh. *British Railways First Generation DMUs*. 2011.
Quick, Michael. *Railway Passenger Stations in Great Britain: A Chronology*. 2009.
RCTS. *A Detailed History of British Railways Standard Steam Locomotives: Volume Four The 9F 2-10-0 Class*. 2008.
RCTS. *Locomotives of the Great Western Railway Parts 1-12*. 1951-1974.
Summerson, Stephen. *Midland Railway Locomotives Volume Four: Johnson Classes Part II (Goods and Later Passenger Tender Engines), Deeley, Fowler and LTSR Classes*. 2005.
Sixsmith, Ian. *The Book of the Ivatt Class 4 2-6-0s*. 2012.
Townsin, Ray. *The Jubilee 4-6-0s*. 2006.
Walmsley, Tony. *Shed by Shed: Part One London Midland*. 2010.
Walmsley, Tony. *Shed by Shed: Part Six: Western*. 2009.